Where in the world is Egypt?

Most of Egypt lies in the **continent** of Africa. However, the eastern region of Egypt, the Sinai **Peninsula**, is situated in the continent of Asia.

To the east of Egypt is the state of Israel and the Red Sea, to the south is Sudan, to the west is Libya and to the north is the Mediterranean sea.

Egypt is four times as big as the United Kingdom. However, 95 per cent of the land is desert, so people cannot live there. This means that most of the population is squeezed into 3 per cent of the country's land area.

▼ Egypt and its place in the world.

Egypt

The national flag of Egypt.

Did you know?

Official name
Arab Republic of E

Location
North east Afric

Surrounding c   ies
Sudan, Libya, State of Israel

Surrounding seas
Mediterranean Sea, Red Sea

Length of coastline 2450km

Capital city Cairo

Area 1 001 500km^2

Population 70 300 000

Life expectancy Male: 63, female: 66

Religions Islam (94%), Christian (6%)

Official language Arabic (English and French widely understood by the educated classes)

Climate Desert. Hot, dry summers with moderate winters

Highest mountains
Mount Katherine (2629m)
Mount Sinai (2285m)

Major river
River Nile (length: 1450km in Egypt; total length of Nile: 6670km)

Currency Egyptian pound

What is Egypt like?

A land in the desert

Travelling through Egypt you will see a mixture of old and new; mud-brick villages and ancient ruins surrounded by modern city buildings of glass and steel. Some people will be wearing jeans or suits, others traditional robes.

River Nile

The Nile flows through the entire length of the country from south to north. On either side of the river lie green strips of rich farmland. These are surrounded by vast deserts.

The Western Desert

To the west of the River Nile is the arid Western Desert, which covers two thirds of Egypt. It is a low-lying area of endless sand and **sand dunes**, stony plains and rocky **plateaux**.

The Eastern Desert

This desert is also known as the Arabian Desert. It lies to the east of the River Nile. Most of the Eastern Desert is uninhabited, but there are a few settlements along the Red Sea

◀ This desert canyon in Sinai contains spectacular natural rock sculptures.

▼ There are two islands on the Nile in Cairo, which are linked to the mainland by bridges. Roda (Rawdah) island is shown below; the other is Zamalik. (Gezira).

Contents

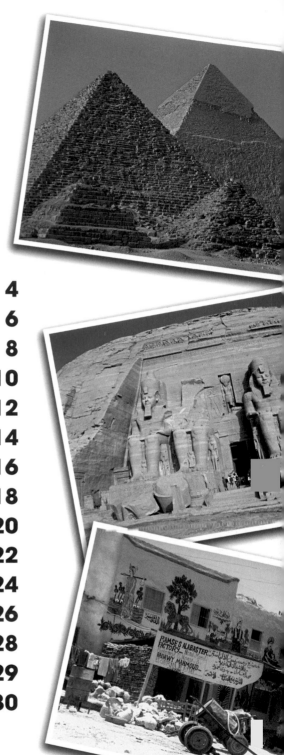

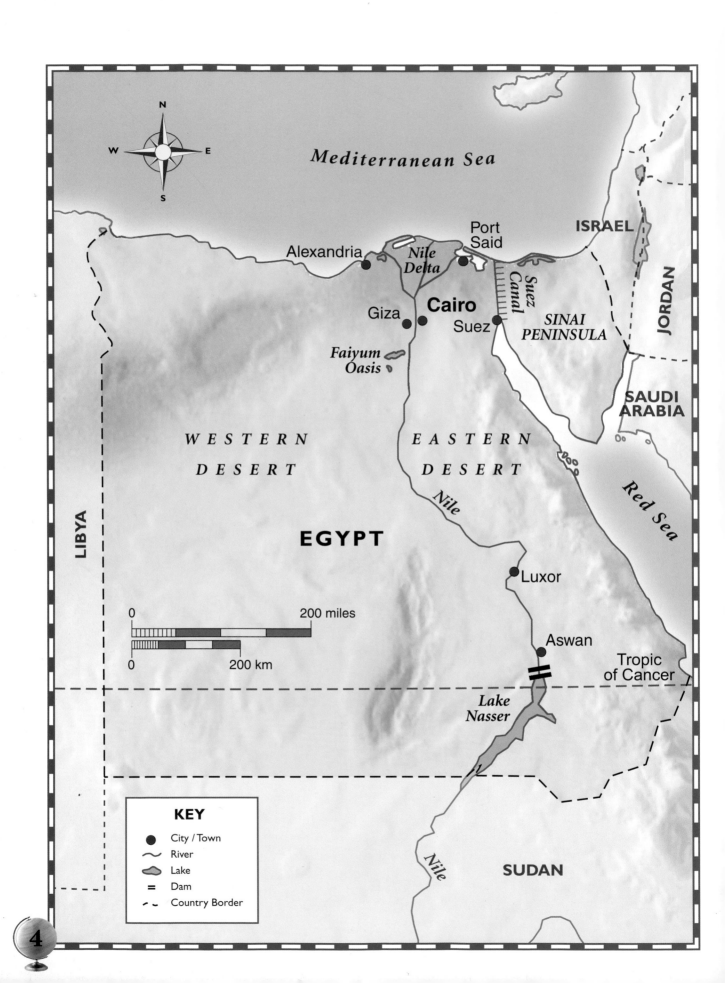

Mediterranean Sea

ISRAEL

Port
Said

Alexandria

*Nile
Delta*

Cairo

Giza

Suez

*Suez
Canal*

*SINAI
PENINSULA*

JORDAN

*Faiyum
Oasis*

SAUDI
ARABIA

*W E S T E R N
D E S E R T*

*E A S T E R N
D E S E R T*

Nile

*Red
Sea*

LIBYA

EGYPT

Luxor

0   200 miles

0   200 km

Aswan

Tropic
of Cancer

*Lake
Nasser*

KEY

● City / Town
〜 River
▬ Lake
= Dam
⌇ Country Border

Nile

SUDAN

coast to the east. Some people live here around the wells and springs to be near a source of water.

Green areas in the desert

In the desert there are areas of land where plants and trees grow well and lakes are formed. These areas are called **oases** and are important for farming.

▶ This young girl is selling shells at Lake Qurun, in the Faiyum Oasis.

Oliver's dad is living in Egypt for six months. He is working for an Egyptian chemical company. Oliver often receives postcards from the places his dad has visited.

▼ Most of Egypt is covered in desert.

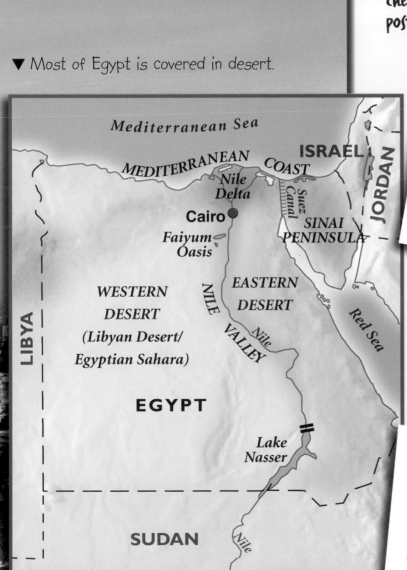

Mediterranean Sea

ISRAEL

MEDITERRANEAN COAST

JORDAN

Nile Delta

Suez Canal

Cairo

SINAI PENINSULA

Faiyum Oasis

EASTERN DESERT

Red Sea

WESTERN DESERT
(Libyan Desert/
Egyptian Sahara)

NILE VALLEY

Nile

LIBYA

EGYPT

Lake Nasser

SUDAN

Nile

Dear Oliver
This postcard shows
Mount Sinai, where God is
thought to have delivered
the Ten Commandments
to Moses. It is on the Sinai
Peninsula. Tomorrow I am
going to Mount Katherine,
Egypt's highest point.
love Dad

Oliver Smith
Broad Bank
Sunny Mead
Wilchester
W18 8CL
ENGLAND

Dear Oliver
This is the Faiyum
Depression in the Western
Desert. It is the most
important oasis in Egypt.
The large freshwater lake
lies 53m below sea level!
love Dad

Oliver Smith
Broad Bank
Sunny Mead
Wilchester
W18 8CL
ENGLAND

Dear Oliver
Today I visited the
Mediterranean Coast.
There are lots of
beautiful white sandy
beaches. Egyptian families
living in Cairo come here to
escape the heat of the
city. Me, too!
love Dad

Oliver Smith
Broad Bank
Sunny Mead
Wilchester
W18 8CL
ENGLAND

Food and drink

Eating in Egypt

Egypt lies at the crossroads where Africa meets Asia. This influences the type of food that Egyptians like to eat.

In Egypt, you will eat meals full of fresh ingredients that are grown in the country. These include different types of beans, such as chickpeas and fava, which are eaten either stewed or ground-up to make pastes like tahini and **houmous**, with lots of garlic. **Okra**, cabbage, aubergines and potatoes are eaten regularly, often stewed with garlic and tomatoes. You will eat lots of tomatoes in Egypt – Egyptians love them! Rice is always available and is even eaten for breakfast.

▼ A weekly vegetable market is held in Qutur village in the Nile Delta.

Meat and fish

Lamb and chicken are the most common meats eaten in Egypt. They are usually grilled or roasted. Shish kebabs, which are pieces of meat and vegetables cooked over a grill on sticks, are extremely popular and are often served with side dishes such as tomato salad and pitta bread. Egyptians also enjoy fish, such as perch and tuna, caught in the Red Sea.

▲ A popular Egyptian family meal of shish kebabs and potatoes.

Dear Oliver
I had a wonderful meal last night. It was Egyptian moussaka with a white cheese topping. The side salad was delicious. It was made with chopped tomato, coriander, mint, some hot green peppers and onions. I ate some hot pitta bread with it. I'll have to make it for you when I get home. I'm eating lots of fresh fruit, such as figs, dates, oranges and pomegranates. Speaking of fruit, there is a great cold drink made from freshly squeezed oranges and sweetened with cut sugar cane. It is just what I need in this hot climate.
Love Dad

Oliver Smith
Broad Bank
Sunny Mead
Wilchester
W18 8CL
ENGLAND

▼ Spice merchants like to **haggle**.

Climate – travelling through the seasons

Hot and dry

No matter what time of year you travel to Egypt, you will probably find it very hot and dry. It is like this for most of the year. During the winter months, December to February, the average daily temperatures are around 13°C in the north and 16°C in the south. In the summer, they are much higher.

▼ The ground in Aswan is dry and parched for most of the year.

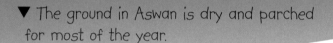

Spring

Between March and April, the khamsin, a hot, dry, dusty wind, blows in from the Western Desert. It can reach a speed of 150km per hour. The sky becomes dark orange and full of dust. Even though everyone shuts their doors and windows tightly, the inside of every house gets covered with sand.

Summer

Summer in Egypt is extremely hot. The temperature is over 31°C most days. The highest temperature recorded in Aswan, in the south of Egypt, was over 50°C! Aswan does not receive much rainfall and is almost bone dry. A lot of water from the Nile and also from Lake Nasser (an artificial lake on the River Nile) evaporates as a result of the extreme heat.

Oliver's dad visited Aswan in July and said it was very hot there. Oliver looked on the Internet to compare the climates in Aswan and Cairo.

CLIMATE DATA FOR ASWAN (°C)											
Jan	Feb	March	April	May	June	July	Aug	Sep	Oct	Nov	Dec
15	17	20	25	30	33	34	33	31	29	23	16
CLIMATE DATA FOR CAIRO (°C)											
Jan	Feb	March	April	May	June	July	Aug	Sep	Oct	Nov	Dec
12	14	16	20	24	27	28	28	25	23	19	14

One night while he was in Aswan, Oliver's dad couldn't sleep. He decided to record the temperature every hour. Here are his records for the 19th of July.

Midnight	01.00	02.00	03.00	04.00	05.00	06.00	07.00	08.00	09.00	10.00	11.00
32°C	31	29	29	28	28	27	27	29	32	34	38
Noon	13.00	14.00	15.00	16.00	17.00	18.00	19.00	20.00	21.00	22.00	23.00
39°C	40	41	41	41	41	40	40	38	36	34	33

Compare these temperatures with those in July in the UK

▼ Traditional wooden boats called feluccas glide gracefully past Aswan.

❓ What sort of clothes would Oliver's dad need for a visit to Aswan?

❓ How would he protect himself from the heat and the sun?

❓ Why do you think many Egyptians wear long flowing white robes?

Getting around Egypt

By air
Egypt's airlines fly to many Egyptian destinations as well as to lots of countries around the world.

By land
Egypt is one of the largest countries in Africa. As you travel around Egypt, you will have many types of vehicles to choose from, including cars, buses, trucks and taxis. Or you can use more old-fashioned forms of transport, such as camels, donkeys and horses.

By rail
Egypt's railway network connects just about every town in the country, from Aswan to Alexandria. Cairo has the only underground system in the whole continent of Africa.

By boat
For centuries, taking a boat on the River Nile was the best way to travel in Egypt. Today, it is possible to take a tourist boat to cruise up the Nile between Aswan and Luxor. Traditional sailboats, called *feluccas*, still travel on the River Nile.

Suez Canal

The Suez Canal is one of the world's busiest shipping routes. It connects the Red Sea and the Mediterranean Sea. The **canal** was dug between 1859 and 1869. Before that, ships bringing cargo by sea to Europe from India and the Far East had to travel around the whole continent of Africa! The canal is 162km long, and the narrowest parts are 60 metres wide.

▼ Ships on the Suez Canal transport goods through Egypt to many countries around the world.

▲ The centre of Cairo is always busy with traffic.

Dear Oliver
I really wanted to take a ride along the River Nile, but not on a tourist boat. So I took a trip on a felucca. Feluccas are traditional Egyptian sailing boats. They rely on the breeze, which builds up during the day, to blow their big cotton sails.
love Dad

Oliver Smith
Broad Bank
Sunny Mead
Wilchester
W18 8CL
ENGLAND

The River Nile

Ten-year-old Mohammed goes to school in Cairo. He is working with two friends on a project about the River Nile.

▲ The River Nile, viewed from the air.

◀ Mohammed's drawing of the Nile shows the countries it flows through.

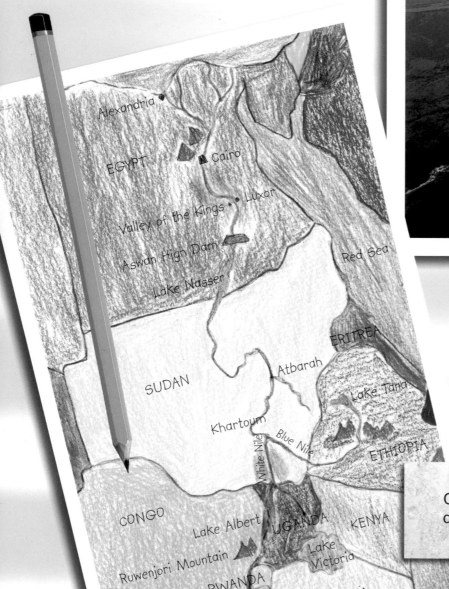

Alexandria

EGYPT

Cairo

Luxor

Valley of the Kings

Aswan High Dam

Lake Nasser

Red Sea

ERITREA

Atbarah

Lake Tana

SUDAN

Khartoum

White Nile

Blue Nile

ETHIOPIA

CONGO

Lake Albert

UGANDA

KENYA

Ruwenjori Mountain

Lake Victoria

RWANDA

BURUNDI

TANZANIA

Lake Tanganyika

Compare the lengths of the Nile and the River Thames in the UK.

By Mohammed, aged 10

From the Nile source to about halfway along its length at Khartoum in Sudan, the river is known as the White Nile. This is because of the milky white colour of the water in the summer. At other times the water is browny-grey and muddy.

At Khartoum the river is joined by the Blue Nile, which starts in the mountains of Ethiopia. This is known as the Blue Nile because it is clear and blue during the months of low water from March to June.

By Layla, aged 10

The River Nile is the world's longest river. It is a truly international river, because it flows through a total of ten countries. It is 6670km long. This is similar to the distance between London and New York!

The water that feeds the Nile starts in the Ruwenzori Mountains, on Uganda's border with the Democratic Republic of Congo, and then collects in Lakes Victoria and Albert before flowing north. The Nile's mouth is in northern Egypt at the Mediterranean Sea.

By Ezzat, aged 9

Before the Blue Nile and the White Nile meet, they flow side by side for several hundred kilometres, not mixing. You can actually see the browny-grey colour of the White Nile and the greeny-blue colour of the Blue Nile. From Khartoum to the Mediterranean Sea only one river, the River Atbarah, joins the Nile. So, unlike most rivers, the River Nile does not get any wider as it nears the sea. Around Cairo, the Nile begins to branch out into its **delta**.

Lake Nasser and the Aswan Dam

Lake Nasser

At the point where the River Nile reaches the border of Sudan and Egypt, the river flows into Lake Nasser, the world's biggest man-made lake.

The Aswan Dam

Lake Nasser was created when the Aswan Dam was built in 1971 to block the flow of the Nile. The **dam** has been described as Egypt's modern pyramid. It is 17 times larger than the biggest pyramid.

▼ Lake Nasser is more than 500km long, of which 150km belong to Sudan and the rest to Egypt.

▼ The Aswan Dam is 3.6km long and 111m high. It is 980m wide at the base and 40m wide at the top.

As part of Mohammed's project on the River Nile, he has recorded the advantages and disadvantages that the building of the Aswan Dam has had on Egypt.

ADVANTAGES AND DISADVANTAGES OF THE ASWAN DAM

ADVANTAGES
1) Controls the flow of the Nile to prevent flooding.
2) Prevents **drought**.
3) Provides a regular supply of water to use for **irrigation**, so crops can be grown all year round.
4) Irrigation increased the amount of land that can be farmed by 30 per cent.
5) Source of energy. The dam produces enough electricity for the whole of Egypt. Its **hydro-electric power** is an energy source that does not create pollution, as oil does.

DISADVANTAGES
1) Thousands of people had to leave their homes to make way for the dam and the lake.
2) Ancient temples and buildings had to be moved, stone by stone, and rebuilt on higher ground.
3) There are fewer fish in the Nile because there are less **nutrients** in the water, since the dam holds back all the **silt**.
4) Farmers have to buy lots of expensive fertilizer (natural or chemical substances that make soil produce more crops), because there is no natural fertilizing of the land by silt.
5) The large number of irrigation **canals** has increased diseases such as malaria (an infectious disease that causes chills and fever), which is spread by mosquitoes that breed in still water.
6) Loss of water through high levels of evaporation from the surface of Lake Nasser.

Farming

Growing food

Egypt is totally dependent on the waters of the River Nile because the country has so little rainfall each year. The river water is used for cooking, washing, drinking and watering **crops**.

The Nile Valley

All along the Nile Valley, a narrow strip of land on each side of the river is farmed. Every available piece of land is **irrigated**, so that Egyptians can grow food to eat and crops to sell.

In the past, farmers relied on the flood water from the river, which left behind rich mud that helped the crops to grow. Now people have to use more irrigation and fertilizers, because the Aswan Dam has stopped the Nile flooding as it used to do.

◀ Tossing dry beans high up in the air in a sieve sifts out all the waste and dust.

▼ Strips of land on both sides of the River Nile are irrigated to grow extra crops.

◀ Some farmers still use traditional methods, such as this sakia wheel to water their land.

In Ezzat's school project, he writes about his family. They are farmers who live in the countryside.

By Ezzat, aged 9

My uncle and grandad are fellahins (farmers) and live in a village about 35km from Cairo. Their land is a few kilometres from the River Nile. They grow wheat, maize and vegetables for the family to eat. They also grow a crop called berseem which they feed to the farm animals. They keep water buffalo, goats and donkeys on the farm. They also grow rice, dates, sugar cane and fruit, such as oranges and bananas, to sell.

My grandad and uncle are lucky, because an irrigation channel (a long ditch) runs next to their fields. They have a pump to lift the water from the channel onto their fields. Some farmers use old methods, such as a shadoof, which is a long pole with a bucket at one end and a weight at the other. The pole is fixed to a post, and the pole swings round so that water from the river can be poured on the fields. Some farmers use animals to turn a wheel called a sakia, which scoops water up and then onto the field.

19

Tourism in Egypt

Historical wonders

The tourist trade is very important to the Egyptian economy. Many tourists visit the River Nile and its surrounding area because this is where Egypt's historical treasures are found.

The ancient Egyptians believed that their time on Earth was short, but that the **afterlife** would go on for ever. They built huge pyramids to use as burial chambers. Tourists are attracted by the age-old mystery of how and why the pyramids were built and thousands visit them each year.

Ancient cities

If you travel to Egypt, you will probably want to visit Giza, a suburb of Cairo. There you will find the Great Pyramids and the huge Sphinx. Luxor, built on the site of the ancient city of Thebes, is another place you could visit.

People have been coming to visit the impressive temples and monuments of Luxor for thousands of years. The Valley of the Kings, including the spectacular tombs of Tutankhamun and Nefertari, is also a big attraction.

▼ The statue of the Sphinx in Giza is 22m high and 50m long. It was built nearly 5000 years ago.

◄ The Great Pyramids are at Giza, on the west bank of the Nile.

Oliver went to stay with his dad in Egypt for the Christmas holidays. He kept a diary of some of the places he visited.

15th December
Today we went to Giza. Wow! I could not believe my eyes! The Sphinx was so huge. The enormous half-human and half-lion statue rose out of the desert, keeping a watchful eye over the three Great Pyramids. I had never seen anything like it before. I was really seeing one of the Seven Wonders of the World.

19th December
Today Dad took me to the Valley of the Kings. We went to Tutankhamun's tomb and looked at the treasures and jewels. They had been buried in his tomb with his mummified body. I knew quite a lot about Tutankhamun because I had done some work on the ancient Egyptians at school.

▲ The great temple at Abu Simbel. This temple had to be moved to higher ground in the 1960s or it would have been flooded after the Aswan Dam was built.

▲ Tutankhamun's gold death mask. Tutankhamun is probably the most famous ancient Egyptian pharaoh, or king. His treasure-filled burial chamber was discovered in 1922.

Egypt's industries

The **textile industry** is the most important industry in Egypt. Other industries include the production of cement, iron and steel, chemicals, fertilizers and rubber products.

Mining has become more important over the last 20 years. Raw materials such as oil and salt are taken out of the ground.

Energy isn't a problem in Egypt. The country is **self-sufficient** in oil, and the Aswan Dam provides most of the country's electrical power.

Agriculture

Even though only four per cent of Egypt's land area can be farmed, agriculture is important. Egypt **imports** about half of its food, because so much of the farmland is used for the production of cotton.

Some crops grown in Egypt are sold around the world. These include maize, sugar cane, wheat, rice, barley, millet (a grass made into grain and animal food), onions, potatoes, tobacco, mangoes, citrus fruits, figs, dates and grapes.

Tourism

The tourist industry is very important to Egypt. The country has always been popular with visitors who are interested in the pyramids and the mysteries of the ancient Egyptian civilization.

▶ A cotton merchant in Cairo stands by huge bales of cotton. Egypt is the world's largest **exporter** of this product.

▼ Nile cruises and trips on feluccas are very popular with tourists.

▶ Making fertilizer is an important industry in Egypt. Much of it is used in Egypt itself, and large amounts are exported to surrounding countries.

Cairo

A mixture of old and new

As you travel around Cairo you will be surprised by the contrasts in the buildings, the methods of transport and even the kind of clothes that people wear. Sometimes you will feel you are in a busy, modern city, and at other times you will feel you have stepped back in history.

Traditional Cairo

Some areas of the city are very traditional. These areas have narrow winding streets, busy markets, covered **bazaars** and craft workshops. There are many tea and coffee houses in these narrow streets. They are very popular.

My name is Ahmed and I live in Cairo, the capital city of Egypt. My city is the largest in Egypt and in the whole of Africa. Nearly 25 per cent of all Egyptians live here.

▼ Cairo's skyline is crowded with modern high-rise buildings and the minarets, or spires, of mosques.

▲ Five million people live in Cairo's camps and slums.

▼ Ali and his friend Adio help out at a copper stall.

Cairo's problems

Some areas of the city are very poor. People live in camps and slums, without any decent water supply or **sewage** system. Many people make a living by collecting rubbish from the streets, sorting through it and selling the materials to be recycled.

Cairo has many problems that face **urban** areas all over the world, such as overcrowding, traffic congestion, air pollution, unemployment and not enough good-quality housing.

My name is Ali. I go to school, but only for half days. This is because there are so many children that the school cannot give us all full-time education. I love to play football and go for bike rides. My dad drives a tourist bus and my mum works in our home.

Travelling through Egyptian cities

As you travel through Egyptian cities, you will be amazed at the incredible mix of ancient and modern architecture and lifestyles. Egyptian cities, such as Luxor, are sometimes compared to open-air museums with huge numbers of preserved monuments.

However, located not far from these ancient monuments and historic sites are new buildings and some of the most up-to-date industries. Today, all aspects of modern life can be found in Egypt's cities.

▼ Along its route, the Suez Canal flows through three lakes.

▼ The city of Alexandria once had a lighthouse that was one of the Seven Wonders of the World.

▼ The hydro-electric power station at Aswan provides electricity for all of Egypt.

My name is Manal and I live in Port Said. This is a **port** on the Mediterranean Sea at the entrance to the Suez Canal. It is the second largest port in Egypt and it's also a fuelling point for ships using the canal. I love to watch the big boats going past. Egyptian products such as cotton and rice are exported from Port Said.

For their school projects, three Egyptian children have written about their home towns. They say what makes their towns special, and what they like to do there for fun.

My name is Elham and I live in Alexandria in northern Egypt. My town is on the Mediterranean Sea, so the climate is cooler than in central Egypt. I am lucky because I can go down to the beach for a swim. My uncle, aunt and cousin Ahmed, who live in Cairo, have a holiday villa here in Alexandria, right on the waterfront. We have lots of fun playing on the sandy beaches. There are lots of hotels and apartments in Alexandria for tourists.
Alexandria is also Egypt's leading port and is a modern industrial city.

My name is Rashid. I live in the city of Suez at the southern end of the Suez Canal. Suez is a fuelling station for ships and a centre for storing oil. Oil is sent by pipelines to Cairo and Alexandria. Petroleum products, paper and fertilizers are made in Suez. My friends and I like to watch the ships refuelling.

Glossary

afterlife
life after death

bazaar
a market, often covered

canal
a man-made water channel for navigation or irrigation

continent
one of the seven large areas of land on the Earth's surface: Africa, Asia, Australasia, Antarctica, North America, South America, Europe

crop
a plant grown for food or raw materials

dam
a man-made barrier across a river, which blocks its flow and creates a lake behind it

delta
the area of flat land at the mouth of a river, which is criss-crossed by many small channels

drought
period when no rain falls

exports
goods and produce sold to another country

haggle
good-natured bargaining about a price

houmous
paste made from chick peas and tahini

hydro-electric power (HEP)
electricity made from the controlled flow of water

imports
goods brought into a country from abroad

industry
making things in factories or workshops

irrigation
taking water onto land from a river, using a system of canals and channels

nutrients
nourishing vitamin and mineral substances

oasis (plural, **oases)**
fertile place in the desert where there is water, and trees grow

okra
green vegetable also called 'ladies' fingers'

peninsula
land surrounded on three sides by water

plateau (plural **plateaux)**
a wide, level stretch of land high above sea-level

port
a place where ships stop to load and unload their cargo and passengers

sand dunes
rounded ridges of drifted sand

self-sufficient
able to provide for oneself

sewage
waste liquid from house toilets or factories

silt
fine fragments of soil and rock carried down by a river

source
where a river or stream starts

textile
fabric or cloth, usually woven

urban
living in, or situated in, a large town or city

Index

Teaching ideas and activities for children

The following activities address and develop the geographical 'enquiry' approach, and promote thinking skills and creativity. The activities in section A have been devised to help children to develop higher order thinking, based on Bloom's taxonomy of thinking. The activities in section B have been devised to promote different types of learning styles, based on Howard Gardner's theory of multiple intelligences.

A: ACTIVITIES TO DEVELOP THINKING SKILLS

ACTIVITIES TO PROMOTE RESEARCH AND RECALL OF FACTS
Ask the children to:
• make an alphabet book for a young child, reflecting what places in Egypt are like (for example, physical and man-made features, weather, industry).
• research and investigate a desert environment. Ask the children to present their information on a poster or in a photo diary.

ACTIVITIES TO PROMOTE UNDERSTANDING
• Ask the children to use this book and other non-fiction books, CD-ROMs and the Internet to find out about farming and industry in Egypt, and then use this information to make a children's TV documentary programme.

ACTIVITIES TO PROMOTE THE USE OF KNOWLEDGE AND SKILLS TO SOLVE PROBLEMS
Ask the children to:
• work in groups to produce a poster advertising different types of holidays to Egypt.
• make notes to explain why the Nile Valley is so heavily populated but other areas of Egypt are not. List the attributes of the River Nile.

ACTIVITIES TO ENCOURAGE ANALYTICAL THINKING
• Ask the children to reflect on what the issues would be if Egypt's population doubled within the next five years.

ACTIVITIES TO PROMOTE CREATIVITY

Ask the children to:

• make a representation of the desert areas through painting or collage.

• design an itinerary for a cruise ship on the River Nile, including on-board activities and onshore excursions to places of interest.

ACTIVITIES TO HELP CHILDREN USE EVIDENCE TO FORM OPINIONS AND EVALUATE CONSEQUENCES OF DECISIONS

Ask the children to:

• rank the places in Egypt they would like to visit in order of preference, giving reasons why.

• write a report, giving reasons, about who in Egypt benefited from the building of the Aswan Dam and who did not.

B: ACTIVITIES BASED ON DIFFERENT LEARNING STYLES

ACTIVITIES FOR LINGUISTIC LEARNERS

Ask the children to:

• write a rap to promote a cruise on the River Nile as a great holiday.

• write a journalistic report about the impact of too many tourists visiting the pyramids.

ACTIVITIES FOR LOGICAL AND MATHEMATICAL LEARNERS

Ask the children to:

• find out about the population of Egypt or Cairo over the past ten years, to collate this information and represent it in a number of graphical ways.

• find ways of graphically representing the information about climate in this book.

ACTIVITIES FOR VISUAL LEARNERS

Ask the children to:

• design a poster or a cartoon to show a visit to the pyramids and a ride on a camel.

• select one place in Egypt and design a visually appealing poster, with a slogan, that could be used to advertise that place.

• draw their favourite place in Egypt on the front of a postcard-sized piece of card.

ACTIVITIES FOR KINAESTHETIC LEARNERS

Ask the children to:

• make a model of the River Nile from its source to the mouth.

• design and build a model of a pyramid, a temple or the Sphinx.

ACTIVITIES FOR MUSICAL LEARNERS

Ask the children to:

• create an Egyptian dance.
• create a short radio advertisement and radio station jingle to advertise a place or tourist attraction in Egypt.

ACTIVITIES FOR INTER-PERSONAL LEARNERS

Ask the children to:

• write a letter to a child living in Cairo, explaining their own lifestyle (school, friends, hobbies and local area).
• plan a visit to Egypt for their family.

ACTIVITIES FOR INTRA-PERSONAL LEARNERS

Ask the children to:

• describe what they feel it would be like to live in Aswan.
• describe how they would feel riding a camel.

ACTIVITIES FOR NATURALISTIC LEARNERS

Ask the children to:

• make notes about the pros and cons of expanding farmland into the desert through the use of irrigation and underground water reservoirs.
• discuss the effect of the Aswan Dam on the plants, animals and fish in the Nile Valley and delta.

LINKS ACROSS THE CURRICULUM

The *Travel Through* series of books offers up-to-date information and cross-curricular opportunities for teaching geography, literacy, numeracy, history, RE, PSHE and citizenship. The series enables children to develop an overview ('the big picture') of each country. This overview reflects the huge diversity and richness of the life and culture of each country. The series aims to prevent the development of misconceptions, stereotypical images and prejudices, which often develop when the focus of a study narrows too quickly onto a small locality within a country. The books in the series help children not only to gain access to this overview, but to develop an understanding of the interconnectedness of places. They contribute to the children's geographical knowledge, skills and understanding, and help them to make sense of the world around them.